BETWEEN

PreK & K

Weekly Reader:
SUMMER EXPRESS

New York • Toronto • London • Auckland • Sydney
Mexico City • New Delhi • Hong Kong • Buenos Aires

Editor: Ourania Papacharalambous
Cover design Tannaz Fassihi and Michelle H. Kim
Interior design by Michelle H. Kim

ISBN: 978-1-338-10888-0
Compilation and illustrations copyright © 2017 by Scholastic Inc.
All rights reserved.
Printed in the U.S.A.
First printing, January 2017.

4 5 6 7 8 9 10   08   23 22 21 20 19 18

Table of Contents

Dear Parent,

Congratulations! You hold in your hands an exceptional educational tool that will give your child a head start in the coming school year.

Inside this book, you'll find 100 practice pages that will help your child review and learn the alphabet, numbers, colors, shapes, sorting, letters, sounds, and so much more! *Weekly Reader: Summer Express* is divided into 10 weeks, with two practice pages for each day of the week, Monday through Friday. However, feel free to use the pages in any order that your child would like. Here are other features you'll find inside:

★ A weekly incentive chart and certificate to motivate and reward your child for his or her efforts.

★ A sheet of colorful stickers to use as weekly rewards.

★ Ideas for fun, skill-building activities you can do with your child any time.

★ Suggestions for creative learning activities that you can do with your child each week.

★ A certificate of completion to celebrate your child's accomplishments.

We hope you and your child will have a lot of fun as you work together to complete this workbook.

Enjoy!

The Editors

Tips for Using This Book

1. Pick a good time for your child to work on the activities. You may want to do it around mid-morning after play, or early afternoon when your child is not too tired.

2. Make sure your child has all the supplies he or she needs, such as pencils and an eraser. Designate a special place for your child to work.

3. Celebrate your child's accomplishments by letting him or her affix stickers to the incentive chart after completing the activities each day. Reward your child's efforts with a bonus sticker at the end of the week as well.

4. Encourage your child to complete the worksheets, but don't force the issue. While you may want to ensure that your child succeeds, it's also important that he or she maintains a positive and relaxed attitude toward school and learning.

5. After you've given your child a few minutes to look over the activity pages he or she will be working on, ask your child to tell you his or her plan of action: "Tell me about what we're doing on these pages." Hearing the explanation aloud can provide you with insights into your child's thinking processes. Can he or she complete the work independently? With guidance? If your child needs support, try offering a choice about which family member might help. Giving your child a choice can help boost confidence and help him or her feel more ownership of the work to be done.

6. When your child has finished the workbook, present him or her with the certificate of completion on page 143. Feel free to frame or laminate the certificate and display it on the wall for everyone to see. Your child will be so proud!

Skill-Building Activities for Any Time

The following activities are designed to complement the 10 weeks of practice pages in this book. These activities don't take more than a few minutes to complete and are just a handful of ways in which you can enrich and enliven your child's learning. Use the activities to take advantage of time you might ordinarily disregard—for example, standing in line at the supermarket. You'll be working to practice key skills and have fun together at the same time.

Find Real-Life Connections

One of the reasons for schooling is to help children function in the real world, to empower them with the abilities they'll truly need. So why not put those developing skills into action by enlisting your child's help with creating a grocery list, reading street signs, sorting pocket change, and so on? He or she can apply reading, writing, science, and math skills in important and practical ways, connecting what he or she is learning with everyday tasks.

An Eye for Patterns

A red-brick sidewalk, a beaded necklace, a Sunday newspaper—all show evidence of structure and organization. You can help your child recognize the way things are structured, or organized, by observing and talking about patterns they see. Your child will apply his or her developing ability to spot patterns across all school subject areas, including alphabet letter formation (writing), attributes of shapes and solids (geometry), and characteristics of narrative stories (reading). Being able to notice patterns is a skill shared by effective readers and writers, scientists, and mathematicians.

Journals as Learning Tools

Most of us associate journal writing with reading comprehension, but having your child keep a journal can help you keep up with his or her developing skills in other academic areas as well—from telling time to matching rhymes. To get started, provide your child with several sheets of paper, folded in half, and stapled together. Explain that he or she will be writing and/or drawing in the journal to complement the practice pages completed each week. Encourage your child to draw or write about what he or she found easy, what was difficult, or what was fun. Before moving on to another set of practice pages, take a few minutes to read and discuss that week's journal entries together.

Promote Reading at Home

- Let your child catch you in the act of reading for pleasure, whether you like reading science fiction novels or do-it-yourself magazines. Store them someplace that encourages you to read in front of your child and **demonstrate that reading is an activity you enjoy**. For example, locate your reading materials on the coffee table instead of your nightstand.

- Set aside a family reading time. By designating a reading time each week, your family is assured an opportunity to discuss with each other what you're reading. You can, for example, share a funny quote from an article. Or your child can tell you his or her favorite part of a story. The key is to **make a family tradition of reading and sharing books** of all kinds together.

- **Put together collections of reading materials** your child can access easily. Gather them in baskets or bins that you can place in the family room, the car, and your child's bedroom. You can refresh your child's library by borrowing materials from your community's library, buying used books, or swapping books and magazines with friends and neighbors.

Skills Alignment

Listed below are the skills covered in the activities throughout *Weekly Reader: Summer Express*. These skills will help children review what they know while helping prevent summer learning loss. They will also better prepare each child to meet, in the coming school year, the math and language arts learning standards established by educators.

Math

	Week 1	Week 2	Week 3	Week 4	Week 5	Week 6	Week 7	Week 8	Week 9	Week 10
Know number names and the count sequence.	✦	✦	✦	✦	✦	✦	✦	✦	✦	✦
Count to tell the number of objects.	✦	✦	✦	✦	✦	✦	✦	✦	✦	✦
Compare numbers.		✦	✦	✦	✦		✦		✦	✦
Understand addition as putting together and adding to.										✦
Understand subtraction as taking apart and taking from.						✦				
Describe and compare measurable attributes.		✦	✦		✦	✦	✦			
Classify objects and count the number of objects in categories.	✦		✦					✦		
Identify and describe shapes.	✦	✦						✦	✦	
Analyze, compare, create, and compose shapes.	✦		✦		✦			✦		

Language Arts

	Week 1	Week 2	Week 3	Week 4	Week 5	Week 6	Week 7	Week 8	Week 9	Week 10
Ask and answer questions about key details in a text or story.		✦	✦	✦		✦	✦	✦	✦	✦
Retell familiar stories, including key details.					✦					
Identify the main topic and retell key details in a text.			✦							
Identify characters, settings, and major events in a story.					✦					
Recognize common types of texts.						✦				✦
Describe relationships in a text or story (e.g., what moment in a story or what person, place, thing or idea in a text, an illustration depicts).		✦				✦	✦		✦	
Compare and contrast the adventures and experiences of characters in a story.								✦		✦
Identify similarities and differences between two texts on the same topic.								✦		
Demonstrate understanding of the organization and basic features of print.	✦	✦	✦	✦	✦	✦	✦	✦	✦	✦
Demonstrate understanding of spoken words, syllables, and sounds (phonemes).		✦	✦	✦	✦	✦	✦	✦		✦
Know and apply grade-level phonics and word analysis skills in decoding words.		✦	✦		✦	✦	✦	✦	✦	✦
Tell about events in the order in which they occur.										✦
Confirm understanding of a text read aloud or information presented orally or through other media.	✦	✦	✦	✦	✦	✦	✦	✦	✦	✦
Demonstrate command of the conventions of standard English grammar and usage when writing or speaking.	✦									

Help Your Child Get Ready: Week 1

Here are some activities that you and your child might enjoy.

Shape Hunt

As your child begins kindergarten, it will be helpful for him or her to know basic shapes—circle, square, triangle, rectangle, oval, diamond—and be able to identify these shapes in the real world. Point to shapes inside and outside the home and ask your child to name the shapes.

Patterns Everywhere!

Patterns are all around us. Being able to recognize these patterns is an essential skill. Help your child find patterns in an article of clothing that a family member is wearing. Alternatively, provide your child with a sheet of paper and crayons and have him or her create a pattern.

Name the Color

When eating colorful foods such as fruits and vegetables, have your child name the colors they see. Continue by asking your child to name the color of favorite fruits and vegetables.

What Letter Am I?

Finger-trace letters on your child's palm or back and have him or her guess what letter you formed.

Art Project!

Make pasta or cereal necklaces with your child to help build fine-motor skills. Provide your child with a length of yarn or lanyard and pasta or cereal with holes in it.

These are the skills your child will be working on this week.

Math

- analyze and compare shapes
- recognize alike and different
- identify patterns
- connect numbers to quantities
- understand number sequence

Handwriting

- numbers *1* and *2*
- number words *one* and *two*
- upper- and lowercase *A* and *B*

Language

- understand antonyms

Incentive Chart: Week 1

Week 1	Day 1	Day 2	Day 3	Day 4	Day 5
Put a sticker to show you completed each day's work.	☆ ☆	☆ ☆	☆ ☆	☆ ☆	☆ ☆

CONGRATULATIONS!

Wow! You did a great job this week!

This certificate is presented to:

_____

_____   _____
Date   Parent/Caregiver's Signature

Matching Kites

Draw a line to match the shape on each child's shirt to a kite.

Circle and Square Search

Draw an X over each circle shape.

Draw a circle around each square shape.

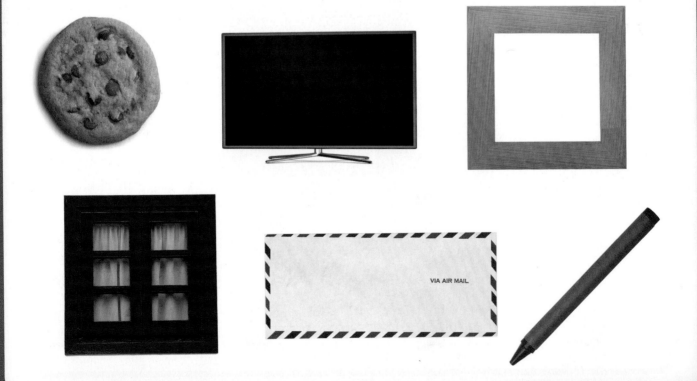

Compare Objects

Circle the object that is different in each box.

Ice Cream Scoop Pattern

Color the last scoop to finish the pattern.

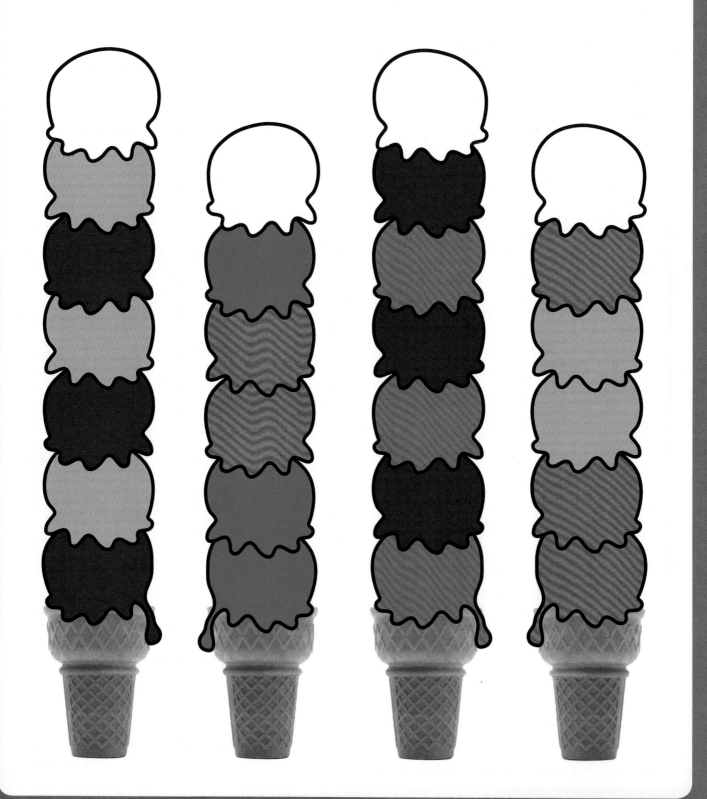

There's only **one** sun

In the sky so blue.

There's only **one** moon.

And there's only **one** you!

Here's how you write the number 1:

Find and circle the things that come in 1's.

Trace the word one.

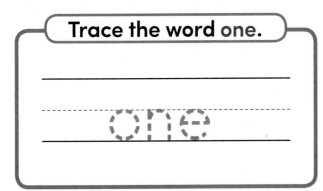

The number that
comes before 1 is:

The number that
comes after 1 is:

2

These **two** peas in a pod
Are so green and so nice.
They always agree
And say everything twice.

Hello!
Hello!

Here's how you write the number 2:

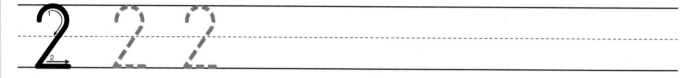

Find and circle the things that come in 2's.

Trace the word two.

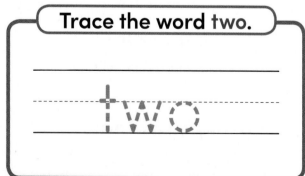

The number that comes before 2 is:

The number that comes after 2 is:

Attention, all!
It's Arnold the Ape.
This amazing athlete
is in tip-top shape.

Trace and write A and a:

Find and circle the A words.

B b

This big bear,
whose name is Ben,
loves berries for breakfast
now and then.

Trace and write B and b:

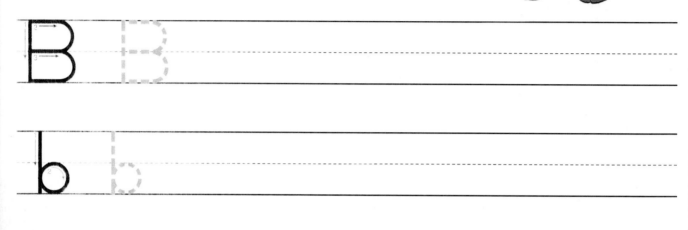

Find and circle the B words.

18

Searching for Opposites

An elephant is big. A mouse is little. **Big** and **little** are opposites.
Circle the picture that shows the opposite.

happy

sad

up

down

boy

girl

fast

slow

Match the Opposites

Match the pictures that are opposites.

hot

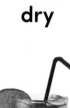

dry

wet

cold

empty

closed

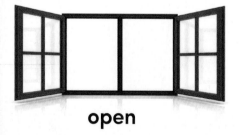

open

full

Help Your Child Get Ready: Week 2

Here are some activities that you and your child might enjoy.

Project Count

Choose an item in your home, such as picture frames or books. Walk around your home with your child and count how many of the item you can find.

Letter Trace

Fill a shallow cake pan with sand or salt. Invite your child to practice tracing the upper- and lowercase letters *A*, *B*, *C*, and *D* with his or her finger.

Where Am I?

Use a box and a smaller item such as a seashell, marble, or leaf. Place the item in different positions and have your child tell you where it is in relation to the box. For example, place a seashell on the box and ask, "Where is the seashell?" (It's *on* the box.) Continue by placing the seashell in different positions and ask your child to tell you where it is.

Simon Says

Play "Simon Says" with your child to introduce the names of different body parts. For example, "Simon says, 'Pat your stomach'" or "Simon says, 'Touch your knees.'"

Jan's New Bike

This is the first of several activities where you will read a story aloud to your child. You may want to read the story more than once. Keep the mood light and your child engaged. As you read, allow your child to look at the image of Jan and Sally. Then read the question aloud. Help your child locate the answer in the picture.

These are the skills your child will be working on this week.

Math

- connect numbers to quantities
- understand number sequence
- compare size
- identify position
- differentiate more vs. fewer
- analyze and compare shapes

Handwriting

- number *3*
- number word *three*
- upper- and lowercase *C* and *D*

Reading & Phonics

- initial consonants: *b*, *p*, and *m*
- identify key details
- make connections between images and a text

Incentive Chart: Week 2

Week 2	Day 1	Day 2	Day 3	Day 4	Day 5
Put a sticker to show you completed each day's work.					

CONGRATULATIONS!

Wow! You did a great job this week!

This certificate is presented to:

_____

_____   _____
Date   Parent/Caregiver's Signature

3

One, two, **three**, GROWL!

This fine family of bears

Has **three** spoons, **three** bowls,

And **three** wooden chairs.

Here's how you write the number 3:

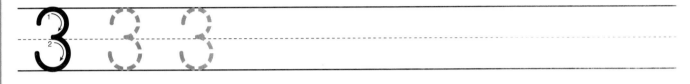

Find and circle the things that come in 3's.

Trace the word three.

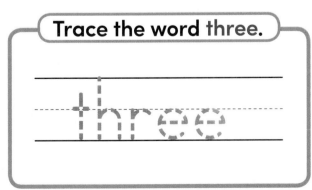

The number that comes before 3 is:

The number that comes after 3 is:

I Can Count to 3!

Write the missing number.

1, 2, _____

Count the number of objects in each box and circle that number.

| 1 2 3 | 1 2 3 | 1 2 3 |

Draw 3 spots on the dog.

Coco the Cow
can cook and bake.
Her favorite dish
is chocolate cake.

Trace and write C and c:

Find and circle the C words.

Deb the Dalmatian
is proud of her spots.
They're round as doorknobs
and domino dots.

Trace and write D and d:

Find and circle the D words.

DOG

Transportation Station

Draw a rectangle around the picture that is big.

Draw an oval around the picture that is small.

In, Out, and All About

Circle the animals that are in their houses.
Draw an X next to the animals that are out of their houses.

Comparing Sets

Compare the sets in each pair. Circle the picture that has **more**.

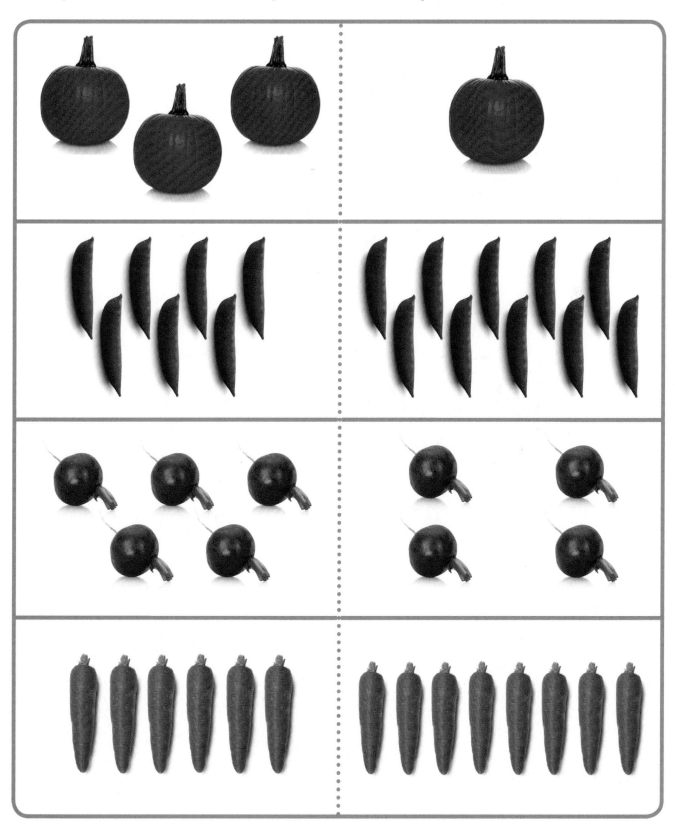

Diamond and Oval Detective

Draw a circle around each diamond shape.

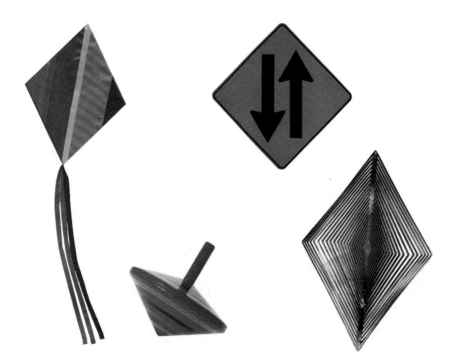

Draw an X next to each oval shape.

Initial Consonants: *b, p, m*

What sound does each letter make?
Circle the pictures that begin with that sound.

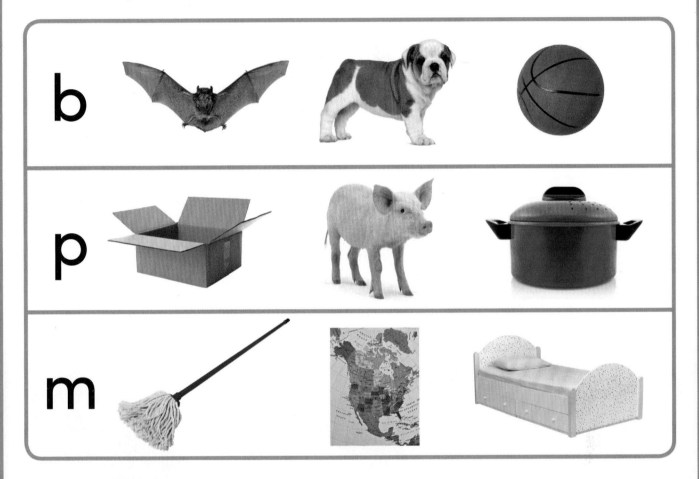

b

p

m

Match each word to its picture.

| bell | pan | mug |

Jan's New Bike

Read the story.

Jan has a new bike. Her new bike is blue. The bike is a birthday present. Jan likes to ride to the park with Sally. Both Jan and Sally wear helmets when they ride.

Circle Jan's bike. What do Jan and Sally wear when they ride? Draw a square around these things in the picture.

Help Your Child Get Ready: Week 3

Here are some activities that you and your child might enjoy.

Build Letters

Provide your child with toothpicks or plastic straws and playdough and encourage your child to use these materials to "build" letters.

Make a Collage!

Provide your child with a large piece of art paper, old magazines, safety scissors, and glue. Have your child make a collage of something he or she is interested in, such as forest animals or sea creatures. Then have your child describe the collage he or she created. Encourage him or her to tell how many of each kind of animal or object was included in the collage.

Shell Sort

At the beach, collect seashells with your child. Later, encourage him or her to sort the shells any way he or she wants. Then ask your child to explain how he or she sorted the shells.

Cloud Shapes

In the park or in your backyard, lie down on the ground with your child and watch the clouds pass by. Call out shapes or figures that you see in the clouds.

Cool Penguins

This is the first of three activities where you will read a piece of informational text to your child. Read the text aloud two to three times. Next, read the directions and the hint to your child. Point to the penguin as you read. Then help your child read each question and the answer choices and circle the correct answers.

These are the skills your child will be working on this week.

Math

- connect numbers to quantities
- understand number sequence
- count objects in groups
- classify objects

Handwriting

- number *4*
- number word *four*
- upper- and lowercase *E, F, G* and *H*

Reading & Phonics

- initial consonants: *t, d,* and *z*
- identify key details

Incentive Chart: Week 3

Week 3	Day 1	Day 2	Day 3	Day 4	Day 5
Put a sticker to show you completed each day's work.	☆ ☆	☆ ☆	☆ ☆	☆ ☆	☆ ☆

CONGRATULATIONS!

Wow! You did a great job this week!

This certificate is presented to:

_____

_____   _____
Date   Parent/Caregiver's Signature

One, two, three, **four**!

Four paws has this kitten.

And each furry paw

Has a warm, fuzzy mitten.

Here's how you write the number 4:

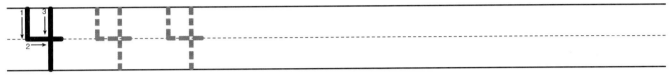

Find and circle the things that come in 4's.

Trace the word four.

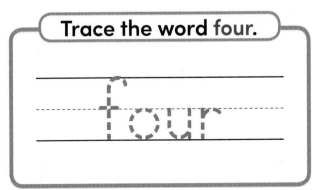

The number that comes before 4 is:

The number that comes after 4 is:

Give the Dogs Spots

Look at the number on the hat. Draw that many spots on the dog.

© Scholastic Inc.

Ee

Eddie the Eagle
has excellent eyes.
Everyone envies
how high he flies.

Trace and write E and e:

Find and circle the E words.

Elm
Street
Mail

Firefly Fifi
flickers her light.
She's a fluttering star
in the forest tonight.

Trace and write F and f:

Find and circle the F words.

3, 4 . . . Let's Read More!

Draw a triangle around each group of 3.
Draw a diamond around each group of 4.

Veggie Graph

Charley picked vegetables for his salad.
Count each kind of vegetable. Then fill in the graph.

Gordon the Goat

is a great and good friend.

He loves giving gifts.

His party won't end!

Trace and write G and g:

Find and circle the G words.

Hh

It's Hallie the Hen.

Hey, hip, hip hooray!

She dances to hip hop

all night and all day!

Trace and write H and h:

Find and circle the H words.

Initial Consonants: *t, d, z*

What sound does each letter make?
Circle the pictures that begin with that sound.

Match each word to its picture.

zip   top   dot

Cool Penguins

Read about penguins.

Penguins are birds. They do not fly. Many penguins live in the South Pole. It is one of the coldest places on Earth. Penguins know how to live in the cold. They have black and white feathers. Their feathers make a warm coat. They also have thick fat to keep them warm.

Fill in the bubble to answer each question.
Hint: One of the questions has two right answers.
Can you find both answers?

1   What animal is the story about?
   ○ owls
   ○ penguins
   ○ parrots

2   Do penguins fly?
   ○ yes
   ○ no
   ○ sometimes

3   Where do many penguins live?
   ○ South Pole
   ○ North Pole
   ○ Alaska

4   How do penguins stay warm?
   ○ furry feet
   ○ thick fat
   ○ feathers

Help Your Child Get Ready: Week 4

Here are some activities that you and your child might enjoy.

What Is It?

Create riddles with your child in order to practice beginning consonant sounds. For example, "It's round and fun to play with. It begins with the *b* sound." (*ball*)

Find the Letter

While reading the newspaper or a magazine, encourage your child to look for words that begin with the same letter as his or her name. Read the words together aloud. Then, ask your child to think of as many words as possible that begin with the same letter.

Letter Art

Give your child chalk to write letters on the sidewalk. Encourage him or her to make the letters as big as possible.

How Many Steps?

Challenge your child to guess how many steps it takes to go from the front door to your kitchen or from the bedroom to the bathroom. Then have your child walk heel-to-toe and count the number of steps. Ask your child: *Do you think it would take more or fewer steps if I (or another grown-up) measured the distance the same way?*

Larry the Frog

Here, your child will practice answering questions about the setting and characters in a story. Read the story to your child. Have him or her look at the picture as you read. Read the text again followed by the questions. Reread the story as necessary to help your child find the correct answer to each question.

These are the skills your child will be working on this week.

Math

- connect numbers to quantities
- understand number sequence
- count objects in groups

Handwriting

- number 5
- number word *five*
- upper- and lowercase *I, J, K* and *L*

Reading & Phonics

- initial consonants: *f, h,* and *v*
- identify key details
- analyze characters

Incentive Chart: Week 4

Week 4	Day 1	Day 2	Day 3	Day 4	Day 5
Put a sticker to show you completed each day's work.	☆ ☆	☆ ☆	☆ ☆	☆ ☆	☆ ☆

CONGRATULATIONS!

Wow! You did a great job this week!

This certificate is presented to:

_____

_____   _____
Date   Parent/Caregiver's Signature

5

A sea star has **five** arms

To wave hello **five** times.

And when he's finished saying hi,

He'll say his **five** good-byes!

Here's how you write the number 5:

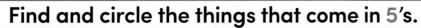

Find and circle the things that come in 5's.

Trace the word five.

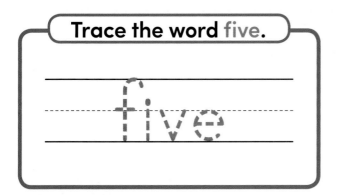

The number that comes before 5 is:

The number that comes after 5 is:

I Can Count to 5!

Write the missing numbers.

1, _____, 3, 4, _____

Count the number of objects in each box and circle that number.

4   5   3   2   4   3   5   2   3

Draw 5 bees around this flower.

Ii

Izzy Iguana's
an incredible fellow.
Most iguanas are green,
but he's red, blue, and yellow.

Trace and write I and i:

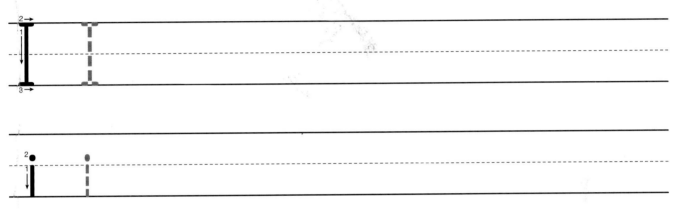

Find and circle the I words.

Jojo the Jaguar
loves driving her jeep.
Here she comes now!
Beep, beep, beep, beep!

Trace and write J and j:

J   J

j   j

Find and circle the J words.

Count With Kites

Look at the number on each child's clothing.
Which kite has the same number of bows?
Draw a line from the child to the correct kite.

Feed the Frog

Help the frogs catch flies. Look at the number on each frog.
Draw a line to the lily pad with the same number of flies.

Kate Kangaroo
gives her kid lots of kisses.
He lives in her pouch,
so she never misses.

Trace and write K and k:

Find and circle the K words.

53

Leo the Lion
loves lemony things.
Licking lollipops makes
him feel like a king.

Trace and write L and l:

Find and circle the L words.

Initial Consonants: *f, h, v*

What sound does each letter make?
Circle the pictures that begin with that sound.

Match each word to its picture.

van   fox   hand

Larry the Frog

Read the story. Then answer each question.

Larry is a frog. Larry is green with brown spots. He loves to play in the pond. Sometimes Larry catches flies. He likes to eat flies for dinner. After Larry catches flies, he hops around the pond.

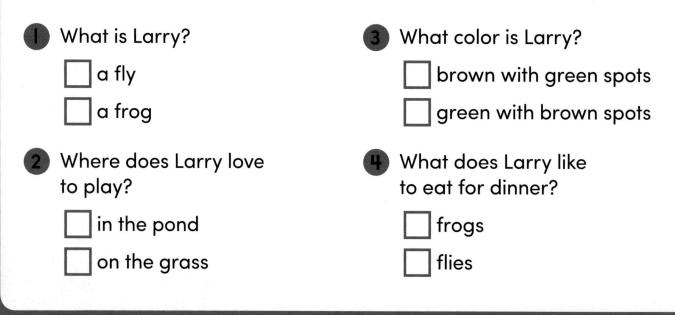

Place an X in the box next to the correct answer.

1 What is Larry?

☐ a fly

☐ a frog

2 Where does Larry love to play?

☐ in the pond

☐ on the grass

3 What color is Larry?

☐ brown with green spots

☐ green with brown spots

4 What does Larry like to eat for dinner?

☐ frogs

☐ flies

Help Your Child Get Ready: Week 5

Here are some activities that you and your child might enjoy.

Bake Time!

Invite your child to help you bake cookies and let him or her help measure the different ingredients using measuring cups and spoons.

More and Fewer?

Play dice with your child to help teach or reinforce the concepts of *more* and *fewer*. Each of you take a die and toss it in turn. Whoever has the die with more dots gets a point. Play for a short time or until someone scores 5 or 10 points.

I Spy

While strolling through the neighborhood or running errands with your child, play "I Spy," calling out letters that you see. For example, "*I spy a big, red letter* M."

Vanishing Letters

At the beach, use a stick to print out your child's name in the sand before the waves come in and wash it away. Then challenge your child to write a letter as many times as possible before the waves return.

Joel's Pets

An important skill for your child is the ability to retell familiar stories. Here, we've included a short story for this purpose. Read the story several times to your child to help him or her become familiar with the story. Then ask your child to identify what's missing in the picture based on the story. Have him or her draw the things that are missing in the picture.

These are the skills your child will be working on this week.

Math

- connect numbers to quantities
- understand number sequence
- differentiate more vs. fewer
- count objects in groups

Handwriting

- number *6*
- number word *six*
- upper- and lowercase *M, N, O* and *P*

Reading & Phonics

- initial consonants: *g, c,* and *j*
- retell familiar stories

Incentive Chart: Week 5

Week 5	Day 1	Day 2	Day 3	Day 4	Day 5
Put a sticker to show you completed each day's work.	☆ ☆	☆ ☆	☆ ☆	☆ ☆	☆ ☆

CONGRATULATIONS!

Wow! You did a great job this week!

This certificate is presented to:

_____

_____   _____
Date   Parent/Caregiver's Signature

Count these eggs
And you'll get **six**.
And in each egg
Is an itty-bitty chick!

Here's how you write the number 6:

Find and circle the things that come in 6's.

Trace the word six.

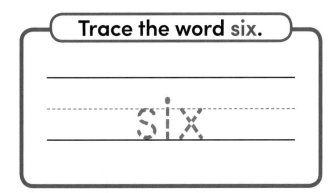

The number that
comes before 6 is:

The number that
comes after 6 is:

More Eggs, Please

In each box, circle the nest with more eggs.

emu eggs

quail eggs

robin eggs

duck eggs

Mm

Marvin the Moose
just loves the museum.
It's full of "M" things.
He's so happy to see them.

Trace and write M and m:

Find and circle the M words.

Nick the Newt

thinks noodles are nice.

He never says "no,"

but "yes" he'll say twice.

Trace and write N and n:

N

n

Find and circle the N words.

5, 6 . . . Flowers to Pick

Draw an oval around each group of 5.
Draw a rectangle around each group of 6.

Which Has More Spots?

For each pair, circle the ladybug with more spots.

Give this ladybug the same number of spots as its friend.

It's Ollie the Octopus.

Give him a hand.

He's the ocean's original

one-man band.

Trace and write O and o:

Find and circle the O words.

Pete the Panda
is proud of his birthday.
Please come to his party,
eat pizza, and play.

Trace and write P and p:

P

p

Find and circle the P words.

Initial Consonants: *g, c, j*

What sound does each letter make?
Circle the pictures that begin with that sound.

g

c

j

Match each word to its picture.

| can | gum | jam |

Joel's Pets

Read the story.

Joel has three pets. He has a cat, a dog, and a bird. Joel's cat is named Fifi. Fifi is gray. Joel's dog is named Hook. Hook is beige with brown stripes. Joel's bird is named Polly. Polly has a red head and a green body. Joel gives them fresh food and water each day.

**Look at Joel's pets below. Draw Hook's missing stripes.
Draw Polly in her bird cage.**

Help Your Child Get Ready: Week 6

Here are some activities that you and your child might enjoy.

Letter Squares

Write each letter of your child's name (first and/or last) on a small square sheet of paper, then put the pieces inside an envelope. Give the letters to your child and have him or her use the letters to create different words.

Numbers to Remember

Help your child memorize important numbers, such as your phone number, *911*, your address, and so on.

Measuring Expedition

Go on a measuring expedition with your child. Pick a nonstandard tool of measurement (such as a pencil or shoe) and measure different things at home, such as the rug, dining table, or bed.

Color Mix

Next time your child wants to paint, offer only the three primary colors (red, blue, and yellow) and encourage your child to experiment with mixing the colors to create new ones.

Mother Nature's Bouquet

It is important for your child to become familiar with different genres. Here we have a poem for you to read to your child. Read the poem several times while your child looks at the picture. Then have him or her identify objects in the picture that are mentioned in the poem.

These are the skills your child will be working on this week.

Math

- connect numbers to quantities
- understand number sequence
- subtraction within 5
- compare size
- identify position
- differentiate fewer vs. more

Handwriting

- upper- and lowercase *Q* and *R*
- number *7*
- number word *seven*

Reading & Phonics

- initial consonants: *w*, *r*, and *y*
- answer questions about details in a text
- make connections between images and a text

Incentive Chart: Week 6

Week 6	Day 1	Day 2	Day 3	Day 4	Day 5
Put a sticker to show you completed each day's work.	☆ ☆	☆ ☆	☆ ☆	☆ ☆	☆ ☆

CONGRATULATIONS!

Wow! You did a great job this week!

This certificate is presented to:

_____

_____ _____
Date   Parent/Caregiver's Signature

7

Look at the sky.

There's a rainbow up there.

With **seven** bright colors,

You can't help but stare!

Here's how you write the number 7:

Find and circle the things that come in 7's.

Trace the word seven.

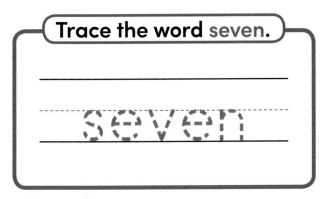

The number that comes before 7 is:

The number that comes after 7 is:

Seed Subtraction

Circle the seeds that remain after the bird eats.

There are 2 seeds

The bird eats 1.

How many are left? _____

There are 3 seeds

The bird eats 2.

How many are left? _____

There are 4 seeds

The bird eats 1.

How many are left? _____

There are 5 seeds

The bird eats 3.

How many are left? _____

Size It Up

Draw a circle around the dog that is short.

Draw a circle around the toy that is short.

Draw a circle around the ruler that is long.

Draw a circle around the pencil that is long.

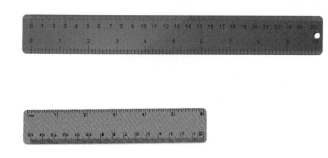

Up on Top

Draw a circle around the cat on the top.

Draw a circle around the girl on top.

Draw a circle around the book on the bottom.

Draw a circle around the bird on the bottom.

Look in a Butterfly Garden

Butterflies drink nectar, the sweet juice in flowers.
That's why they visit flower gardens!
Find and circle these things in the garden.

1 shovel   2 rocks   3 pink flowers   4 caterpillars   5 butterflies

Comparing Sets

Compare the sets in each pair. Circle the picture that has fewer.

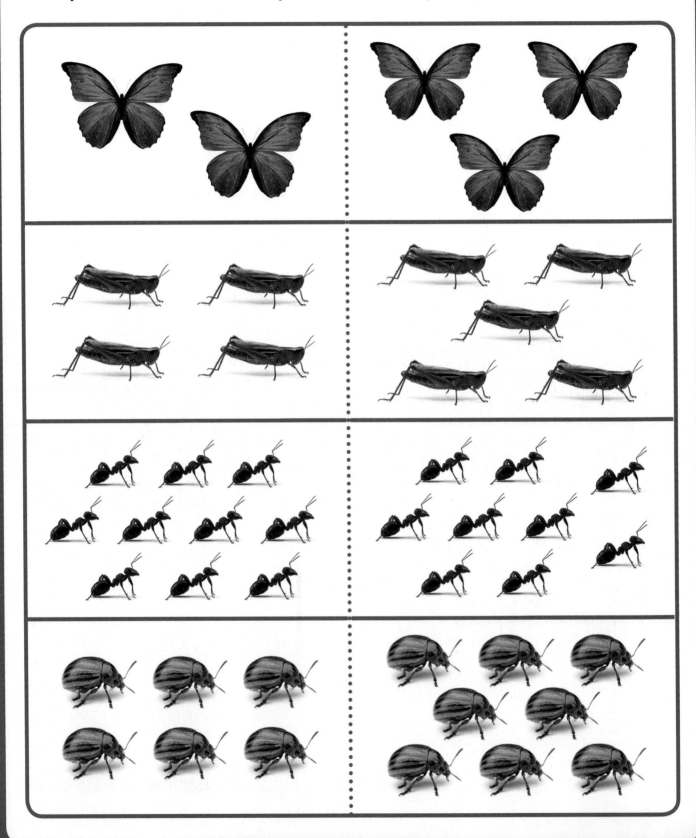

Quinn the Quail
is quite a queen.
She quietly sits
so she can be seen.

Trace and write Q and q:

Find and circle the Q words.

Quack!

Rosie the Rabbit
loves red, red, red.
Red on her paws
and red on her head.

Trace and write R and r:

Find and circle the R words.

Initial Consonants: *w, r, y*

What sound does each letter make?
Circle the pictures that begin with that sound.

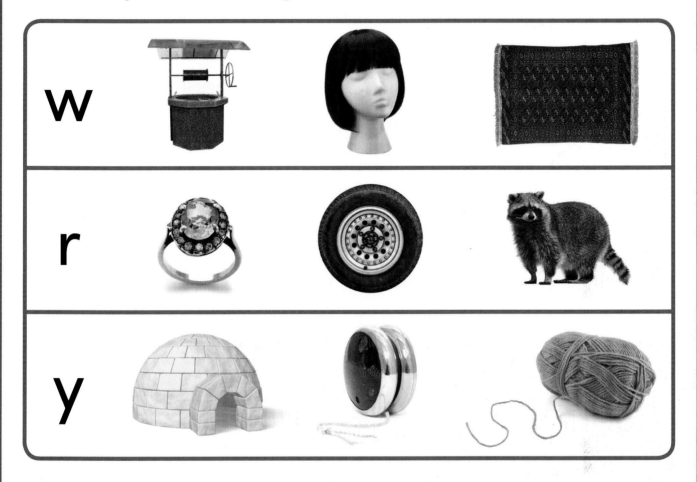

w

r

y

Match each word to its picture.

web   rug   yak

Mother Nature's Bouquet

Read the poem. What things from the poem can you find in the picture? Point to each.

Sweet joy! The flowers have come!

They've followed the showers.

They've grown with the sun.

They've risen up high.

They've spread their leaves.

They've opened their petals
to welcome the bees.

They've brightened the day
in their own sweet way.

They've grown to become
Mother Nature's bouquet!

Help Your Child Get Ready: Week 7

Here are some activities that you and your child might enjoy.

Glittering Letters

Have your child write letters using glue and glitter. Your child can squirt glue on paper to form a letter, then sprinkle glitter on the glue. When the glue dries, your child can finger trace the letters he or she has formed.

Candy Count

When eating colored candy, such as jellybeans, have your child count how many of each color there are in a bag. Then, have your child order the candies from the color with the fewest number to the color with the most.

Find a Letter

While reading a magazine with your child, challenge him or her to find a particular letter, such as the letter T, on the page and circle it.

Writing With Purpose

Let your child sit with you while you write out your grocery list or your list of things to do. This will allow your child to see authentic reasons for writing.

Will and Frank

Here, your child will practice comparing characters. Read each story aloud to your child. Track the print with your finger as you read so that your child can practice making connections between letters and sound. Read the story again and have your child pay careful attention to the picture, then tell you the answers to the questions.

These are the skills your child will be working on this week.

Math

- connect numbers to quantities
- understand number sequence
- count objects in groups
- differentiate fewer vs. more

Handwriting

- number *8*
- number word *eight*
- upper- and lowercase *S, T, U* and *V*

Reading & Phonics

- initial consonants: *s, t,* and *n*
- compare and contrast characters in a story

Incentive Chart: Week 7

Week 7	Day 1	Day 2	Day 3	Day 4	Day 5
Put a sticker to show you completed each day's work.	☆ ☆	☆ ☆	☆ ☆	☆ ☆	☆ ☆

CONGRATULATIONS!

Wow! You did a great job this week!

This certificate is presented to:

_____

_____ _____
Date   Parent/Caregiver's Signature

Look at the octopus!

Isn't he great?

Count his arms

And you'll get **eight**!

Here's how you write the number 8:

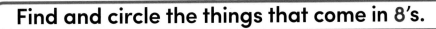

Find and circle the things that come in 8's.

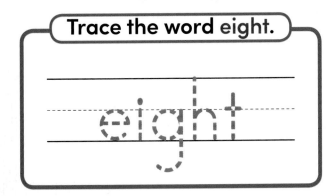

Trace the word eight.

eight

The number that comes before 8 is:

The number that comes after 8 is:

7, 8 . . . Time to Skate

Draw a circle around each group of 7.
Draw a square around each group of 8.

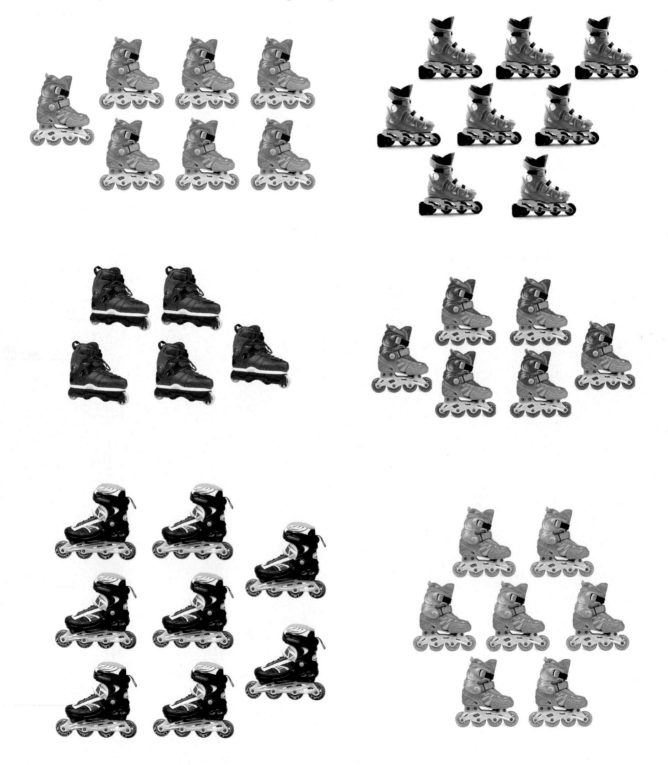

Sammy the Seal
sails out to sea.
Summer's the best.
His friends all agree.

Trace and write S and s:

S

s

Find and circle the S words.

Tt

Tessa the Turtle
loves toast and tea.
She serves them to Toad
on the trunk of a tree.

Trace and write T and t:

Find and circle the T words.

Numbers in the Sea

Find and circle an animal with:

1 curling tail

5 pointy arms

2 clacking claws

6 long tentacles

4 green flippers

8 amazing arms

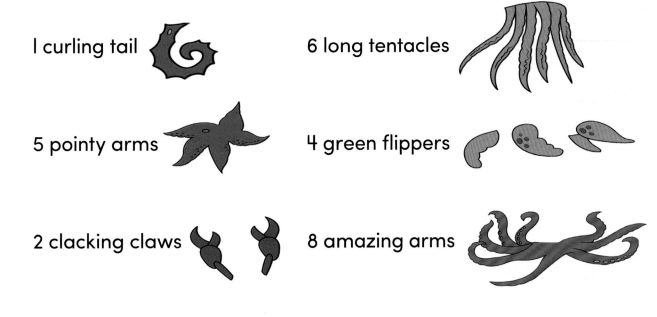

Tasty Snacks

Circle the one with fewer tasty snacks.

Umberto the Unicorn,
how lucky you are,
usually sleeping
under your lucky star.

Trace and write U and u:

Find and circle the U words.

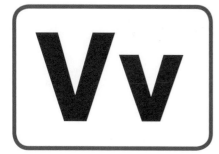

Victor the Vulture
is fond of his view.
There's a valley of violets
and vegetables, too.

Trace and write V and v:

Find and circle the V words.

© Scholastic Inc.

Initial Consonants: *s, t, n*

What sound does each letter make?
Circle the pictures that begin with that sound.

s

t

n

Match each word to its picture.

net   snake   truck

Will and Frank

Read each story. Then answer the questions.

This is Will. He likes to ride his skateboard. Will rides fast. He rides with his friend Frank. Will is not being safe. What does he need to be safe?

This is Frank. He likes to ride his skateboard, too. Frank wears a helmet. He wears knee pads and elbow pads, too. Frank is being safe.

1 How are Will and Frank alike?

2 How are they different?

3 What does Will need to be safe?

Help Your Child Get Ready: Week 8

Here are some activities that you and your child might enjoy.

Build Shapes

Using gumdrops or marshmallows and toothpicks, or ice cream sticks and glue, encourage your child to build different shapes, such as triangles, squares, or rectangles.

Magic Letters

Buy a set of magnetic letters so your child can form words on the refrigerator while you cook.

Kebab Patterns

Enlist your child's help in creating a healthy fruit kebab snack—and practice patterns. Using small wooden skewers and different fruits, have your child make *ABAB* patterns (like banana, strawberry, banana, strawberry) or even *ABCABC* patterns (grape, banana, blueberry, grape, banana, blueberry).

On My Own

Encourage your child to button his or her own shirt, zip his or her own zippers, and tie his or her own shoelaces to build fine-motor skills.

Bats; Birds

An important skill for your child is being proficient in the ability to make comparisons between two texts on the same or similar topics. Here, we have a text about bats and a text about birds. Read each to your child several times. Then read aloud the questions and answer choices. Encourage your child to point out any differences they see in the pictures as well.

These are the skills your child will be working on this week.

Math

- connect numbers to quantities
- understand number sequence
- differentiate more vs. fewer
- classify objects
- analyze and compare shapes

Handwriting

- number *9*
- number word *nine*
- upper- and lowercase *W*, *X*, *Y* and *Z*

Reading & Phonics

- initial consonants: *k*, *l*, and *q*
- compare and contrast two texts
- make connections between images and a text

Incentive Chart: Week 8

Week 8	Day 1	Day 2	Day 3	Day 4	Day 5
Put a sticker to show you completed each day's work.	☆ ☆	☆ ☆	☆ ☆	☆ ☆	☆ ☆

CONGRATULATIONS!

Wow! You did a great job this week!

This certificate is presented to:

_____

_____   _____
Date   Parent/Caregiver's Signature

See the juicy watermelon.

Wow, it looks so nice!

With pink fruit and **nine** seeds—

I really want a slice!

Here's how you write the number 9:

Find and circle the things that come in 9's.

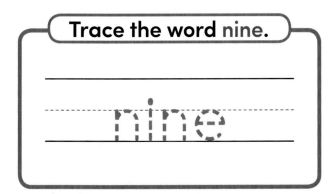

Trace the word nine.

nine

The number that comes before 9 is:

The number that comes after 9 is:

Who Has More?

Circle the animal that has more.

William the Wolf
has wandered out west,
where wagon wheels roll
and the sun comes to rest.

Trace and write W and w:

Find and circle the W words.

How did X-ray Fish get his extra cool name? His see-through body is his claim to fame.

Trace and write X and x:

Find and circle words and things that have an X.

Out of Place

Put an X on the picture that doesn't belong.

Rectangle and Triangle Teasers

Draw an X next to each rectangle shape.

Draw a circle around each triangle shape.

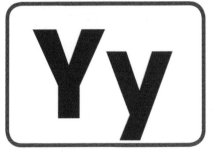

Yolanda the Yak
can never stop yapping.
It's yakkity-yak,
even when she is napping.

Trace and write Y and y:

Find and circle the Y words.

Zelda the Zebra
roams through the zoo,
zipping and zooming,
and zig-zagging, too.

Trace and write Z and z:

Find and circle the Z words.

Initial Consonants: *k, l, q*

What sound does each letter make?
Circle the pictures that begin with that sound.

Match each word to its picture.

lip   key   question

Read each text. Then put an X in the box next to the correct answer.

Birds

Birds have feathers. They also have wings. Most birds use their wings to fly. Birds eat with their beaks. Most birds eat during the day and rest at night.

Bats

Bats have fur. They have wings, too. Bats eat with their teeth. Bats eat at night. They rest during the day. Bats hang upside down when they rest.

1 How are bats and birds alike?

☐ both have wings

☐ both hang upside down

2 How are bats and birds different?

☐ birds have teeth

☐ bats have fur

3 What other way are bats and birds different? Circle the pictures that show the difference.

Help Your Child Get Ready: Week 9

Here are some activities that you and your child might enjoy.

Let's Jump Rope!

As your child plays jump rope, encourage him or her to chant the alphabet, one letter for each jump.

I Can Spell My Name

Help your child write the letters of his or her first name. Together, count the number of letters in your child's name.

Counting Cars

Let your child look out the window and count how many cars or people pass by in 3 to 5 minutes.

Sound Patterns

Play a clapping game with your child to hone his or her listening skills. Clap a simple pattern, such as clap-rest-clap, and ask your child to repeat the pattern back to you. Gradually increase the complexity of the pattern as you continue the game.

Home in a Shell

It is important that your child become adept at identifying and understanding the relationship between visuals and a text. In texts for young children, the visuals usually consist of pictures. As your child gets older, the visuals will also include charts, graphs, and diagrams. Read the text about hermit crabs to your child. Help him or her answer the questions.

These are the skills your child will be working on this week.

Math

- connect numbers to quantities
- understand number sequence
- identify position
- compare objects in groups

Handwriting

- number *10*
- number word *ten*
- upper- and lowercase letters of the alphabet

Reading & Phonics

- high-frequency word *I*
- initial consonants
- make connections between images and a text

Incentive Chart: Week 9

Week 9	Day 1	Day 2	Day 3	Day 4	Day 5
Put a sticker to show you completed each day's work.	☆ ☆	☆ ☆	☆ ☆	☆ ☆	☆ ☆

CONGRATULATIONS!

Wow! You did a great job this week!

This certificate is presented to:

_____

_____ _____
Date   Parent/Caregiver's Signature

10

This cute little baby
Has one button nose,
Plus **ten** teeny fingers
And **ten** wiggly toes!

Here's how you write the number 10:

Find and circle the things that come in 10's.

Trace the word ten.

ten

The number that
comes before 10 is:

Habitat

A habitat is the place an animal lives. Look at a sea horse habitat. Sea horses need plants or coral to hold on to.

Find and circle:

6 **yellow** sea horses

3 **blue** sea horses

I very tiny **pink** sea horse

Did you find all 10 sea horses?
Count them and trace the number:

Above or Below . . . Sure You Know!

Draw a square around the bee **above** the flower.

Draw a square around the ladybug **above** the leaf.

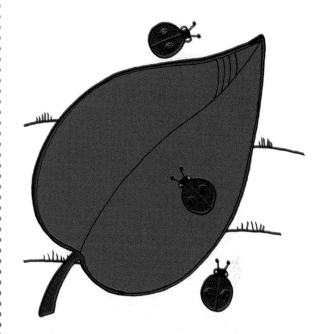

Draw a square around the rabbit **below** the hat.

Draw a square around the doll **below** the table.

I Do Many Things

Circle the word I.

Me

I smile.

I read.

I jump.

I yawn.

I sleep.

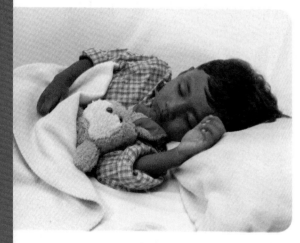

ZZZZZZ . . .

I Can Count to 10!

Write the missing numbers.

1, 2, ___, 4, 5, ___, 7, 8, ___, 10

Count the number of objects in each box and circle that number

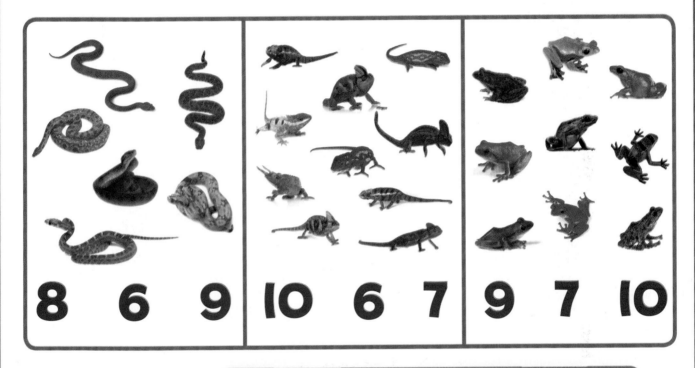

| 8 6 9 | 10 6 7 | 9 7 10 |

Draw 10 fish
in the fish tank.

Just the Same

Draw a line to match the groups with the same number of items.

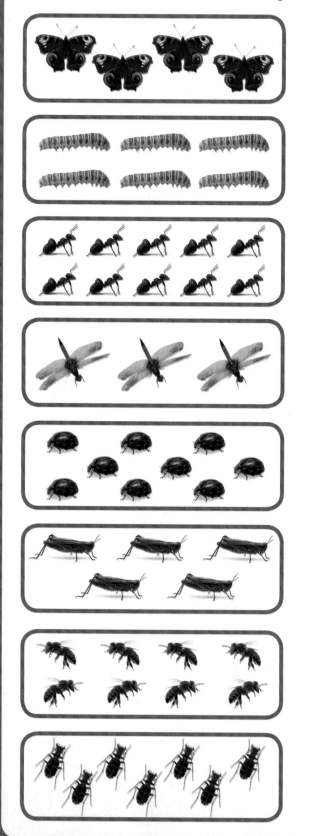
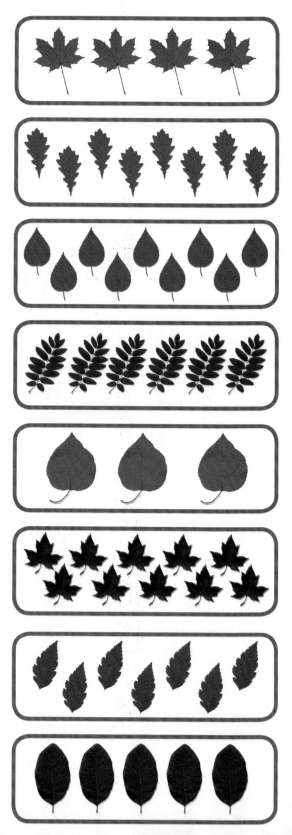

Alphabet Parade

Name the picture. Trace the uppercase and lowercase letter.

A a   B b   C c   D d

E e   F f   G g   H h   I i

J j   K k   L l   M m

Alphabet Parade

Name the picture. Trace the uppercase and lowercase letter.

Initial Consonants

Name each picture. Write the letter it begins with.

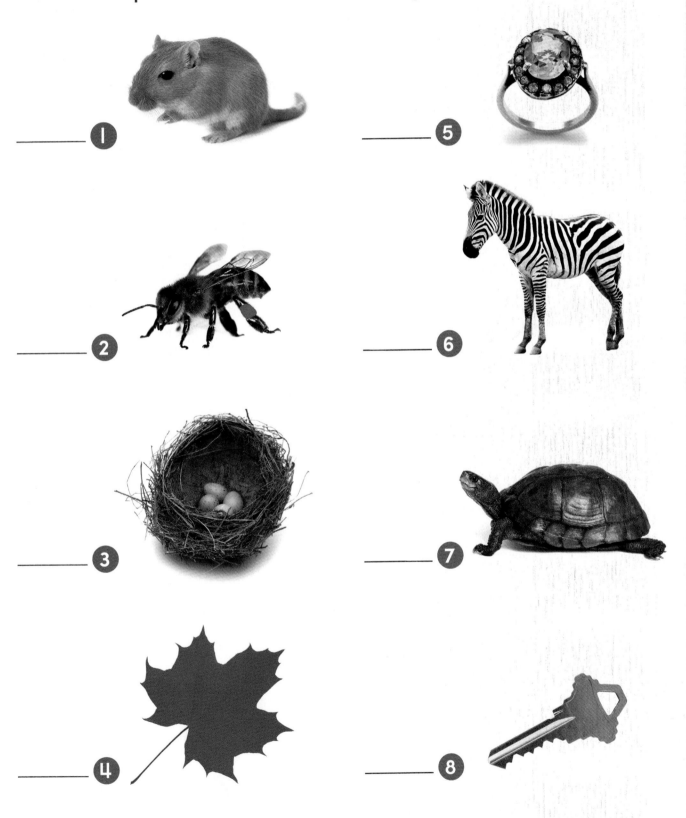

_____ 1

_____ 2

_____ 3

_____ 4

_____ 5

_____ 6

_____ 7

_____ 8

Home in a Shell

Read about hermit crabs. Then answer each question.

Hermit crabs have ten legs. Some live on land along the shore. Some live in water. Hermit crabs borrow seashells. They make the seashells their home. Hermit crabs carry their homes everywhere. When a hermit crab grows, it finds a bigger seashell.

Check the box next to the correct answer.

1 Where is the hermit crab in the picture?

☐ on land along the shore

☐ in the water

2 What do hermit crabs carry everywhere?

☐ other hermit crabs

☐ their seashells

3 How many legs does a hermit crab have? Circle the number.

1   2   3   4   5   6   7   8   9   10

Help Your Child Get Ready: Week 10

Here are some activities that you and your child might enjoy.

Word of the Day

Make a list of high-frequency words—words that appear frequently in the English language—such as *the, to, and, a, he, I, you, it, of, in, was, said, that, she, for*, and so on. Pick a word of the day and have your child point out that word every time he or she sees it.

Button Sort

Gather a collection of buttons and invite your child to sort the buttons by different attributes. For example, your child can sort the buttons by color, by the number of holes, and so on.

How Much?

Give your child coins to sort. Help him or her identify each coin and how much it is worth.

Nature's Patterns

Next time you go to the park with your child, bring some paper and crayons or pencils, and make rubbings of tree trunks, leaves, and so on.

Summer Fun

Here, your child is exposed to two genres, a poem and a story, and is asked to make comparisons between them. Read the poem and the story aloud to your child several times. Then read the questions to your child. Reread the texts as needed. Help your child answer the questions.

These are the skills your child will be working on this week.

Math

- identify sequence
- addition within 5
- connect numbers to quantities

Reading & Phonics

- identify words that rhyme
- high-frequency words: *see* and *a*
- differentiate letters and numbers
- compare two texts

Incentive Chart: Week 10

Week 10	Day 1	Day 2	Day 3	Day 4	Day 5
Put a sticker to show you completed each day's work.	☆ ☆	☆ ☆	☆ ☆	☆ ☆	☆ ☆

CONGRATULATIONS!

Wow! You did a great job this week!

This certificate is presented to:

_____

_____   _____
Date   Parent/Caregiver's Signature

Rhyme Time

Rhyming words have the same ending sound. Say the name of each picture. Circle the two pictures that rhyme in each row.

Perfect Order

Write l by what happens first.
Write 2 by what happens second.
Write 3 by what happens third.

Time for Rhymes

Say the name of each picture.
Circle the two pictures that rhyme in each group.

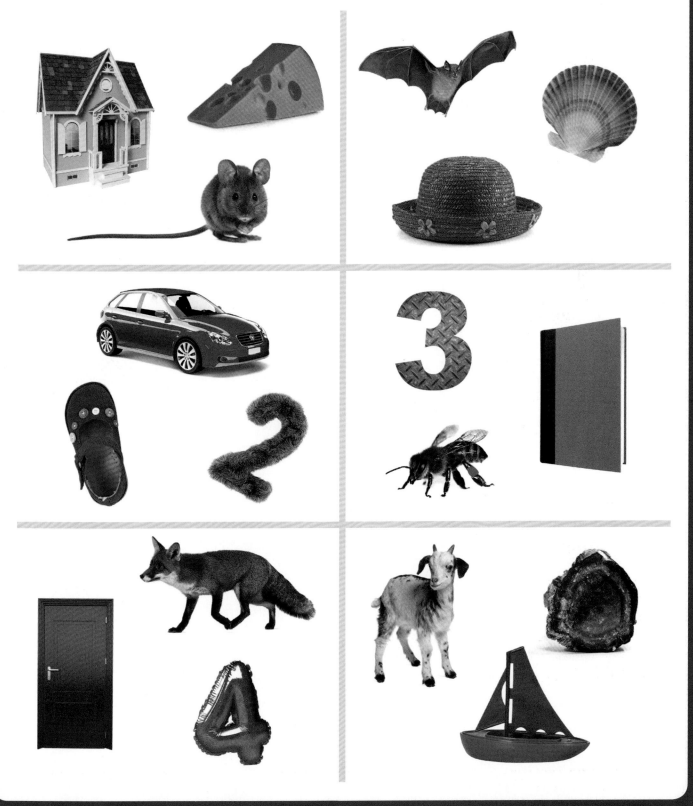

I See the Animals

Circle the word see.

I see the elephant.

I see the lion.

I see the zebra.

I see the bee.

I see the animals.

The animals see me!

Classify

Draw a circle around each number.
Draw an X through each letter.

7	p	f	4
h	2	10	k
s	n	5	a
v	d	o	9
y	r	3	m
8	t	b	6

Plenty of Pumpkins

How many pumpkins? Count and write your answer on the line.

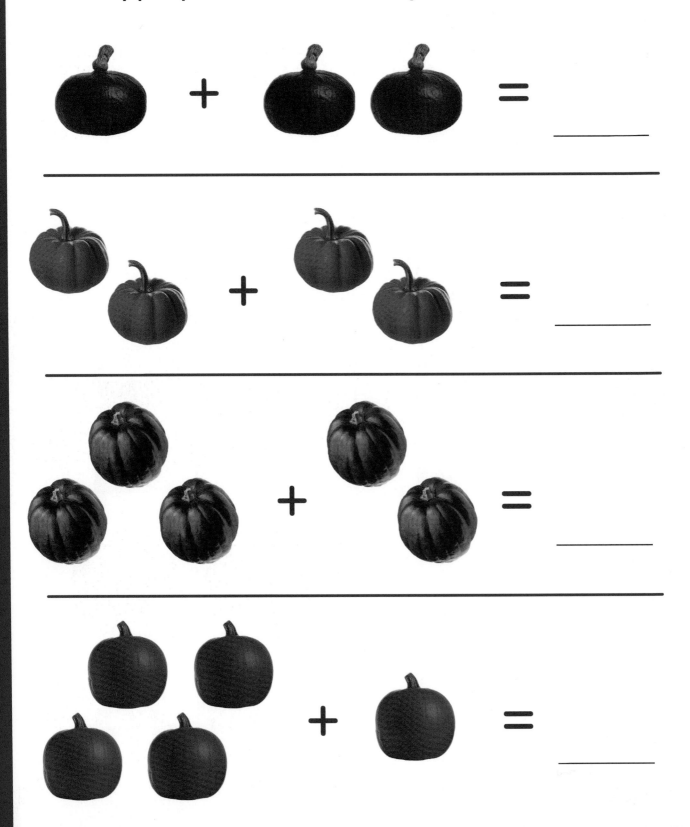

Shapely Sets

Draw a line to match each number to the set of shapes.

More Shapely Sets

Draw a line to match each number to the set of shapes.

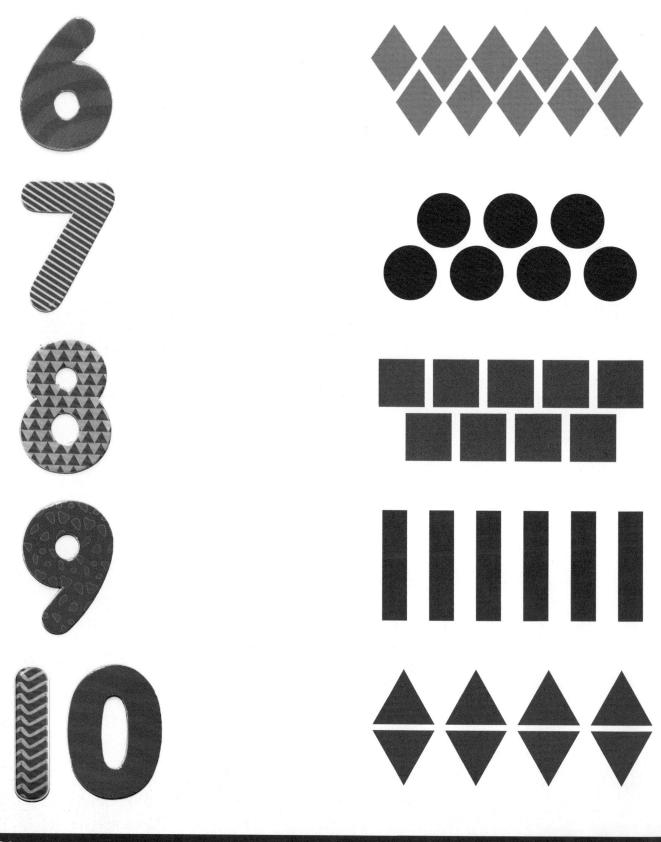

A Park

Circle the word A.

A boy.

A girl.

A swing.

A sandbox.

A slide.

A park.

Come play!

Summer Fun

Read the poem and the story. Then answer the questions.

Poem

Jean, it's Labor Day!

The sun is shining bright today.

Won't you come out to play?

Yes, Dan. But Mom says to be okay

I must wear sunscreen while I play.

Story

It was a hot and sunny Labor Day. Evan wanted to go out to play. It was the last holiday before school. He put on his sunscreen and a hat. Then he went to play with his friends.

1. What does Dan want?

2. What does Evan do before he goes out to play?

3. How are the poem and the story alike?

Answer Key

Week 1

Matching Kites

Draw a line to match the shape on each child's shirt to a kite.

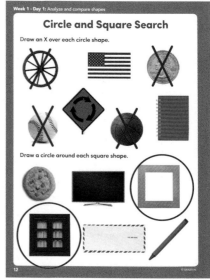

Circle and Square Search

Draw an X over each circle shape.

Draw a circle around each square shape.

Compare Objects

Circle the object that is different in each box.

Ice Cream Scoop Pattern

Color the last scoop to finish the pattern.

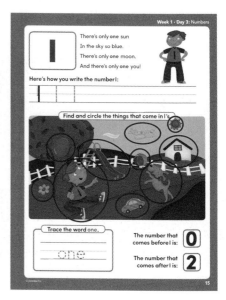

1

There's only one sun
In the sky so blue.
There's only one moon.
And there's only one you!

Here's how you write the number 1:

Find and circle the things that come in 1's.

Trace the word one.

one

The number that comes before 1 is: **0**

The number that comes after 1 is: **2**

2

These **two** peas in a pod
Are so green and so nice.
They always agree
And say everything twice.

Hello!
Hello!

Here's how you write the number 2:

Find and circle the things that come in 2's.

Trace the word two.

two

The number that comes before 2 is: **1**

The number that comes after 2 is: **3**

Aa

Attention, all!
It's Arnold the Ape.
This amazing athlete
is in tip-top shape.

Trace and write A and a:

A

a

Find and circle the A words.

Bb

This big bear,
whose name is Ben,
loves berries for breakfast
now and then.

Trace and write B and b:

B

b

Find and circle the B words.

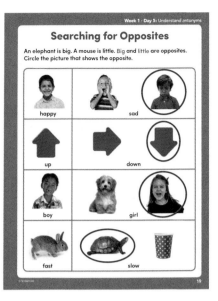

Searching for Opposites

An elephant is big. A mouse is little. Big and little are opposites.
Circle the picture that shows the opposite.

happy	sad
up	down
boy	girl
fast	slow

19

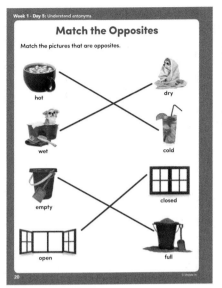

Match the Opposites

Match the pictures that are opposites.

hot — dry
wet — cold
empty — closed
open — full

20

Week 2

3

One, two, three, GROWL!
This fine family of bears
Has three spoons, three bowls,
And three wooden chairs.

Here's how you write the number 3:

3 3 3

Find and circle the things that come in 3's.

Trace the word three.

three

The number that comes before 3 is: **2**

The number that comes after 3 is: **4**

23

I Can Count to 3!

Write the missing number.

1, 2, __3__

Count the number of objects in each box and circle that number.

1 (2) 3   (1) 2 3   1 2 (3)

Draw 3 spots on the dog.

24

Cc

Coco the Cow can cook and bake. Her favorite dish is chocolate cake.

Trace and write C and c:

C C

c c

Find and circle the C words.

25

Dd

Deb the Dalmatian is proud of her spots. They're round as doorknobs and domino dots.

Trace and write D and d:

D D

d d

Find and circle the D words.

26

Transportation Station

Draw a rectangle around the picture that is big.

Draw an oval around the picture that is small.

27

In, Out, and All About

Circle the animals that are in their houses.
Draw an X next to the animals that are out of their houses.

29

131

Comparing Sets

Compare the sets in each pair. Circle the picture that has more.

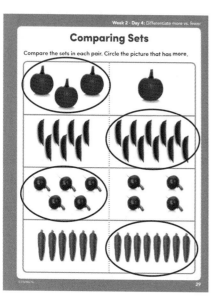

Diamond and Oval Detective

Draw a circle around each diamond shape.

Draw an X next to each oval shape.

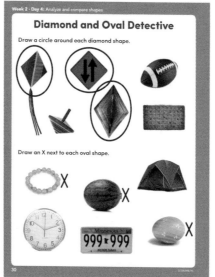

Initial Consonants: *b, p, m*

What sound does each letter make?
Circle the pictures that begin with that sound.

b

p

m

Match each word to its picture.

bell   pan   mug

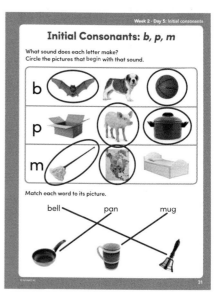

Jan's New Bike

Read the story.

Jan has a new bike. Her new bike is blue. The bike is a birthday present. Jan likes to ride to the park with Sally. Both Jan and Sally wear helmets when they ride.

Circle Jan's bike. What do Jan and Sally wear when they ride? Draw a square around these things in the picture.

Week 3

4

One, two, three, four!
Four paws has this kitten.
And each furry paw
Has a warm, fuzzy mitten.

Here's how you write the number 4:

4 4 4

Find and circle the things that come in 4's.

Trace the word four.

four

The number that comes before 4 is: **3**

The number that comes after 4 is: **5**

Give the Dogs Spots

Look at the number on the hat. Draw that many spots on the dog.

Ee

Eddie the Eagle
has excellent eyes.
Everyone envies
how high he flies.

Trace and write E and e:

E

e

Find and circle the E words.

Ff

Firefly Fifi
flickers her light.
She's a fluttering star
in the forest tonight.

Trace and write F and f:

F

f

Find and circle the F words.

132

3, 4 . . . Let's Read More!

Draw a triangle around each group of 3.
Draw a diamond around each group of 4.

39

Veggie Graph

Charley picked vegetables for his salad.
Count each kind of vegetable. Then fill in the graph.

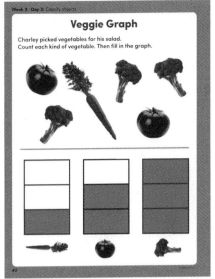

40

Gg

Gordon the Goat
is a great and good friend.
He loves giving gifts.
His party won't end!

Trace and write G and g:

G G

g g

Find and circle the G words.

41

Hh

It's Hallie the Hen.
Hey, hip, hip hooray!
She dances to hip hop
all night and all day!

Trace and write H and h:

H H

h h

Find and circle the H words.

42

Initial Consonants: *t, d, z*

What sound does each letter make?
Circle the pictures that begin with that sound.

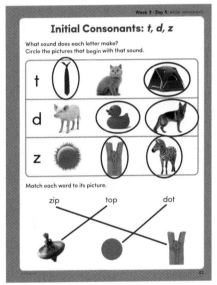

Match each word to its picture.

zip   top   dot

43

Cool Penguins

Read about penguins.

Penguins are birds. They do not fly. Many penguins live in the South Pole. It is one of the coldest places on Earth. Penguins know how to live in the cold. They have black and white feathers. Their feathers make a warm coat. They also have thick fat to keep them warm.

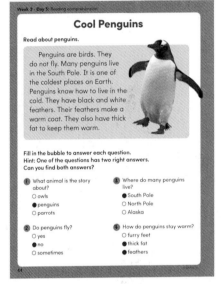

Fill in the bubble to answer each question.
Hint: One of the questions has two right answers.
Can you find both answers?

1. What animal is the story about?
   ○ owls
   ● penguins
   ○ parrots

2. Do penguins fly?
   ○ yes
   ● no
   ○ sometimes

3. Where do many penguins live?
   ● South Pole
   ○ North Pole
   ○ Alaska

4. How do penguins stay warm?
   ○ furry feet
   ● thick fat
   ● feathers

44

Week 4

5

A sea star has five arms
To wave five times.
And when he's finished saying hi,
He'll say his five good-byes!

Here's how you write the number 5:

5 5 5

Find and circle the things that come in 5's.

Trace the word five.

five

The number that comes before 5 is: 4

The number that comes after 5 is: 6

47

I Can Count to 5!

Write the missing numbers.

1, **2**, 3, 4, **5**

Count the number of objects in each box and circle that number.

④ 5 3   2 4   ③ ⑤ 2 3

Draw 5 bees around this flower.

48

Ii

Izzy Iguana's
an incredible fellow.
Most iguanas are green,
but he's red, blue, and yellow.

Trace and write I and i:

I

i

Find and circle the I words.

49

Jj

Jojo the Jaguar
loves driving her jeep.
Here she comes now!
Beep, beep, beep, beep!

Trace and write J and j:

J

j

Find and circle the J words.

50

Count With Kites

Look at the number on each child's clothing.
Which kite has the same number of bows?
Draw a line from the child to the correct kite.

4   2   5   3

51

Feed the Frog

Help the frogs catch flies. Look at the number on each frog.
Draw a line to the lily pad with the same number of flies.

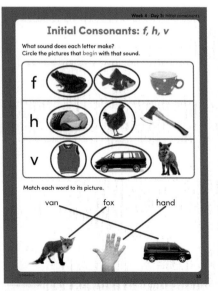

52

Kk

Kate Kangaroo
gives her kid lots of kisses.
He lives in her pouch,
so she never misses.

Trace and write K and k:

K

k

Find and circle the K words.

53

Ll

Leo the Lion
loves lemony things.
Licking lollipops makes
him feel like a king.

Trace and write L and l:

L

l

Find and circle the L words.

54

Initial Consonants: f, h, v

What sound does each letter make?
Circle the pictures that begin with that sound.

f

h

v

Match each word to its picture.

van   fox   hand

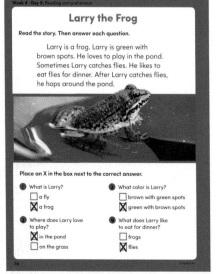

55

Larry the Frog

Read the story. Then answer each question.

Larry is a frog. Larry is green with
brown spots. He loves to play in the pond.
Sometimes Larry catches flies. He likes to
eat flies for dinner. After Larry catches flies,
he hops around the pond.

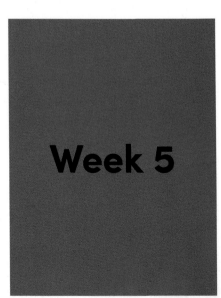

Place an X in the box next to the correct answer.

1 What is Larry?
☐ a fly
☒ a frog

2 Where does Larry love
to play?
☒ in the pond
☐ on the grass

3 What color is Larry?
☐ brown with green spots
☒ green with brown spots

4 What does Larry like
to eat for dinner?
☐ frogs
☒ flies

56

Week 5

134

6

Count these eggs
And you'll get six.
And in each egg
Is an itty-bitty chick!

Here's how you write the number 6:

6 6 6

Find and circle the things that come in 6's.

Trace the word six.

six

The number that comes before 6 is: **5**

The number that comes after 6 is: **7**

More Eggs, Please

In each box, circle the nest with more eggs.

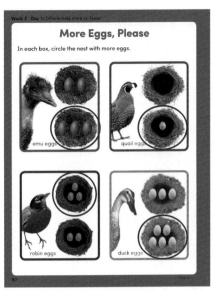

emu eggs
quail eggs
robin eggs
duck eggs

Mm

Marvin the Moose
just loves the museum.
It's full of "M" things,
He's so happy to see them.

Trace and write M and m:

M M

m m

Find and circle the M words.

Nn

Nick the Newt
thinks noodles are nice.
He never says "no,"
but "yes" he'll say twice.

Trace and write N and n:

N N

n n

Find and circle the N words.

5, 6 . . . Flowers to Pick

Draw an oval around each group of 5.
Draw a rectangle around each group of 6.

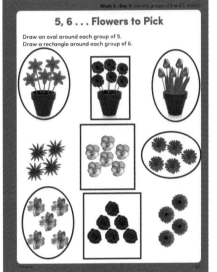

Which Has More Spots?

For each pair, circle the ladybug with more spots.

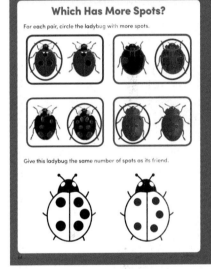

Give this ladybug the same number of spots as its friend.

Oo

It's Ollie the Octopus.
Give him a hand.
He's the ocean's original
one-man band.

Trace and write O and o:

O O

o o

Find and circle the O words.

Pp

Pete the Panda
is proud of his birthday.
Please come to his party,
eat pizza, and play.

Trace and write P and p:

P P

p p

Find and circle the P words.

Initial Consonants: *g, c, j*

What sound does each letter make?
Circle the pictures that begin with that sound.

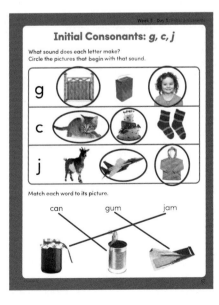

g

c

j

Match each word to its picture.

can   gum   jam

Joel's Pets

Read the story.

Joel has three pets. He has a cat, a dog, and a bird. Joel's cat is named Fifi. Fifi is gray. Joel's dog is named Hook. Hook is beige with brown stripes. Joel's bird is named Polly. Polly has a red head and a green body. Joel gives them fresh food and water each day.

Look at Joel's pets below. Draw Hook's missing stripes. Draw Polly in her bird cage.

Week 6

7

Look at the sky.
There's a rainbow up there.
With seven bright colors,
You can't help but stare!

Here's how you write the number 7:

7

Find and circle the things that come in 7's.

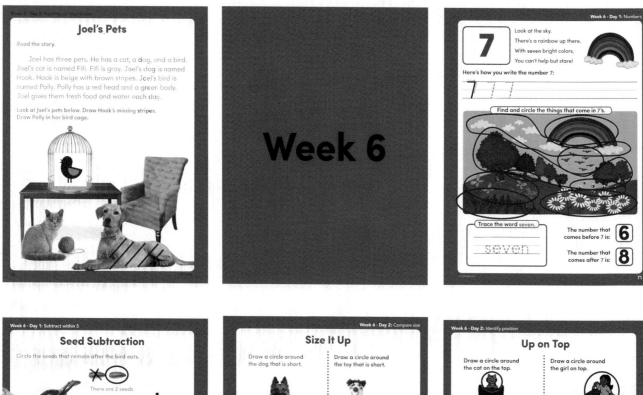

Trace the word seven.

seven

The number that comes before 7 is: **6**

The number that comes after 7 is: **8**

Seed Subtraction

Circle the seeds that remain after the bird eats.

There are 2 seeds
The bird eats 1.
How many are left? **1**

There are 3 seeds
The bird eats 2.
How many are left? **1**

There are 4 seeds
The bird eats 1.
How many are left? **3**

There are 5 seeds
The bird eats 3.
How many are left? **2**

Size It Up

Draw a circle around the dog that is short.

Draw a circle around the toy that is short.

Draw a circle around the ruler that is long.

Draw a circle around the pencil that is long.

Up on Top

Draw a circle around the cat on the top.

Draw a circle around the girl on top.

Draw a circle around the book on the bottom.

Draw a circle around the bird on the bottom.

Look in a Butterfly Garden

Butterflies drink nectar, the sweet juice in flowers. That's why they visit flower gardens! Find and circle these things in the garden.

1 shovel   2 rocks   3 pink flowers   4 caterpillars   5 butterflies

Comparing Sets

Compare the sets in each pair. Circle the picture that has fewer.

Qq

Quinn the Quail
is quite a queen.
She quietly sits
so she can be seen.

Trace and write Q and q:

Q Q

q q

Find and circle the Q words.

Quack!

Rr

Rosie the Rabbit
loves red, red, red.
Red on her paws
and red on her head.

Trace and write R and r:

R R

r r

Find and circle the R words.

78

Initial Consonants: w, r, y

What sound does each letter make?
Circle the pictures that begin with that sound.

w			
r			
y			

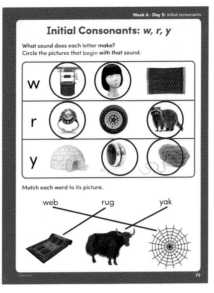

Match each word to its picture.

web   rug   yak

79

Mother Nature's Bouquet

Read the poem. What things from the poem can you find
in the picture? Point to each.

Sweet joy! The flowers have come!
They've followed the showers.
They've grown with the sun.
They've risen up high.
They've spread their leaves.

**Your child should point to the
sun, flowers, leaves, flower
petals, and bees.**

They've grown to become
Mother Nature's bouquet!

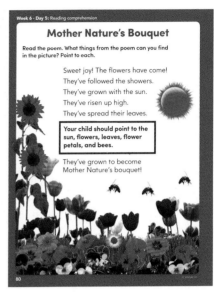

80

Week 7

8

Look at the octopus!
Isn't he great?
Count his arms
And you'll get **eight**!

Here's how you write the number 8:

8 8 8

Find and circle the things that come in 8's.

Trace the word eight.

eight

The number that
comes before 8 is: **7**

The number that
comes after 8 is: **9**

83

7, 8 . . . Time to Skate

Draw a circle around each group of 7.
Draw a square around each group of 8.

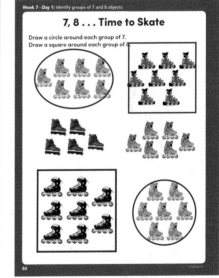

84

Ss

Sammy the Seal
sails out to sea.
Summer's the best.
His friends all agree.

Trace and write S and s:

S S

s s

Find and circle the S words.

85

Tt

Tessa the Turtle
loves toast and tea.
She serves them to Toad
on the trunk of a tree.

Trace and write T and t:

T T

t t

Find and circle the T words.

86

Numbers in the Sea

Find and circle an animal with:

1 curling tail	6 long tentacles
5 pointy arms	4 green flippers
2 clacking claws	8 amazing arms

87

Tasty Snacks

Circle the one with fewer tasty snacks.

88

Uu

Umberto the Unicorn,
how lucky you are,
usually sleeping
under your lucky star.

Trace and write U and u:

U

u

Find and circle the U words.

89

Vv

Victor the Vulture
is fond of his view.
There's a valley of violets
and vegetables, too.

Trace and write V and v:

V V

v v

Find and circle the V words.

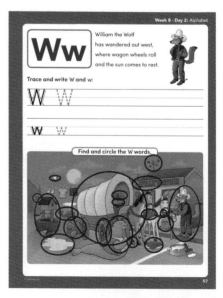

90

Initial Consonants: s, t, n

What sound does each letter make?
Circle the pictures that begin with that sound.

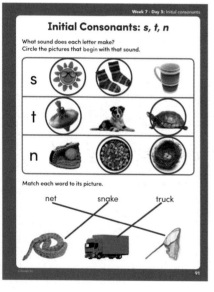

s			
t			
n			

Match each word to its picture.

net   snake   truck

Will and Frank

Read each story. Then answer the questions.

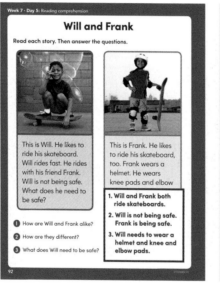

This is Will. He likes to ride his skateboard. Will rides fast. He rides with his friend Frank. Will is not being safe. What does he need to be safe?

This is Frank. He likes to ride his skateboard, too. Frank wears a helmet. He wears knee pads and elbow

1. Will and Frank both ride skateboards.
2. Will is not being safe. Frank is being safe.
3. Will needs to wear a helmet and knee and elbow pads.

1 How are Will and Frank alike?
2 How are they different?
3 What does Will need to be safe?

92

Week 8

9

See the juicy watermelon.
Wow, it looks so nice!
With pink fruit and nine seeds—
I really want a slice!

Here's how you write the number 9:

9 9 9

Find and circle the things that come in 9's.

Trace the word nine.

nine

The number that comes before 9 is: [8]

The number that comes after 9 is: [10]

Who Has More?

Circle the animal that has more.

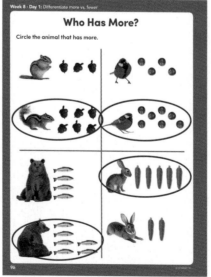

96

Ww

William the Wolf
has wandered out west,
where wagon wheels roll
and the sun comes to rest.

Trace and write W and w:

W W

w w

Find and circle the W words.

97

Xx

How did X-ray Fish get his extra cool name? His see-through body is his claim to fame.

Trace and write X and x:

X X

x x

Find and circle words and things that have an X.

98

Out of Place

Put an X on the picture that doesn't belong.

99

Rectangle and Triangle Teasers

Draw an X next to each rectangle shape.

Draw a circle around each triangle shape.

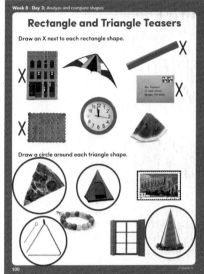

100

Yy

Yolanda the Yak can never stop yapping. It's yakkity-yak, even when she is napping.

Trace and write Y and y:

Y Y

y y

Find and circle the Y words.

101

Zz

Zelda the Zebra roams through the zoo, zipping and zooming, and zig-zagging, too.

Trace and write Z and z:

Z Z

z z

Find and circle the Z words.

102

Initial Consonants: k, l, q

What sound does each letter make?
Circle the pictures that begin with that sound.

k

l

q

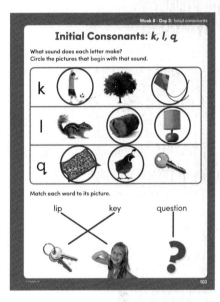

Match each word to its picture.

lip   key   question

103

Read each text. Then put an X in the box next to the correct answer.

Birds

Birds have feathers. They also have wings. Most birds use their wings to fly. Birds eat with their beaks. Most birds eat during the day and rest at night.

Bats

Bats have fur. They have wings, too. Bats eat with their teeth. Bats eat at night. They rest during the day. Bats hang upside down when they rest.

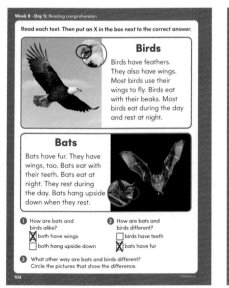

❶ How are bats and birds alike?
[X] both have wings
[ ] both hang upside down

❷ How are bats and birds different?
[ ] birds have teeth
[X] bats have fur

❸ What other way are bats and birds different? Circle the pictures that show the difference.

104

Week 9

10

This cute little baby Has one button nose, Plus ten teeny fingers And ten wiggly toes!

Here's how you write the number 10:

10 10 10

Find and circle the things that come in 10's.

Trace the word ten.

ten

The number that comes before 10 is: **9**

107

139

Habitat

A habitat is the place an animal lives. Look at a sea horse habitat. Sea horses need plants or coral to hold on to.

Find and circle:
6 **yellow** sea horses
3 **blue** sea horses
I very tiny pink sea horse

Did you find all I0 sea horses?
Count them and trace the number:

Above or Below . . . Sure You Know!

Draw a square around the bee above the flower.

Draw a square around the ladybug above the leaf.

Draw a square around the rabbit below the hat.

Draw a square around the doll below the table.

I Do Many Things

Circle the word I.

Me

I smile.

I read.

I jump.

I yawn.

I sleep.

zzzzzzz . . .

I Can Count to I0!

Write the missing numbers.

I, 2, **3**, 4, 5, **6**, 7, 8, **9**, I0

Count the number of objects in each box and circle that number

8 (6) 9   (10) 6 7   (9) 7 I0

Draw I0 fish in the fish tank.

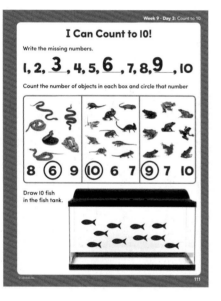

Just the Same

Draw a line to match the groups with the same number of items.

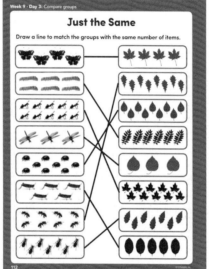

Alphabet Parade

Name the picture. Trace the uppercase and lowercase letter.

Check your child's work.

Aa Bb Cc Dd

Ee Ff Gg Hh Ii

Jj Kk Ll Mm

Alphabet Parade

Name the picture. Trace the uppercase and lowercase letter.

Check your child's work.

Nn Oo Pp Qq

Rr Ss Tt Uu Vv

Ww Xx Yy Zz

Initial Consonants

Name each picture. Write the letter it begins with.

M 1   R 5

B 2   Z 6

N 3   T 7

L 4   K 8

Home in a Shell

Read about hermit crabs. Then answer each question.

Hermit crabs have ten legs. Some live on land along the shore. Some live in water. Hermit crabs borrow seashells. They make the seashells their home. Hermit crabs carry their homes everywhere. When a hermit crab grows, it finds a bigger seashell.

Check the box next to the correct answer.

1 Where is the hermit crab in the picture?
☑ on land along the shore
☐ in the water

2 What do hermit crabs carry everywhere?
☐ other hermit crabs
☑ their seashells

3 How many legs does a hermit crab have? Circle the number.
I 2 3 4 5 6 7 8 9 (I0)

Week 10

Rhyme Time

Rhyming words have the same ending sound. Say the name of each picture. Circle the two pictures that rhyme in each row.

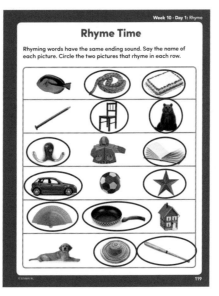

Perfect Order

Write 1 by what happens first.
Write 2 by what happens second.
Write 3 by what happens third.

Time for Rhymes

Say the name of each picture.
Circle the two pictures that rhyme in each group.

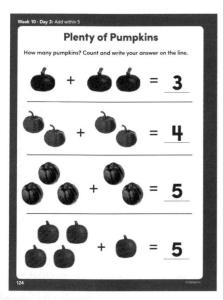

I See the Animals

Circle the word see.

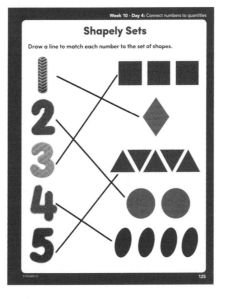

I see the elephant.
I see the lion.
I see the zebra.
I see the bee.
I see the animals.
The animals see me!

Classify

Draw a circle around each number.
Draw an X through each letter.

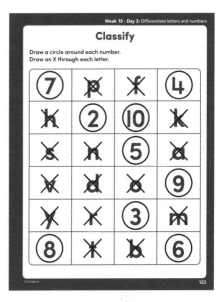

Plenty of Pumpkins

How many pumpkins? Count and write your answer on the line.

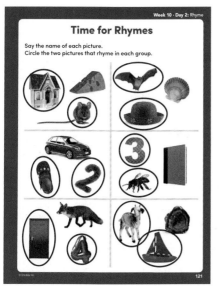

Shapely Sets

Draw a line to match each number to the set of shapes.

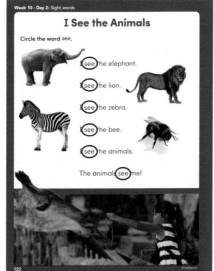

More Shapely Sets

Draw a line to match each number to the set of shapes.

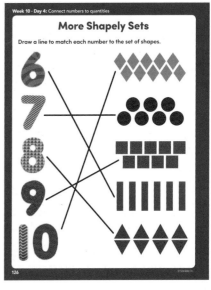

A Park

Circle the word A.

Ⓐ boy.

Ⓐ girl.

Ⓐ swing.

Ⓐ sandbox.

Ⓐ slide.

Ⓐ park.

Come play!

© Scholastic, Inc.

127

Summer Fun

Read the poem and the story. Then answer the questions.

Poem

Jean, it's Labor Day!

The sun is shining bright today.

Won't you come out to play?

Yes, Dan. But Mom says to be okay

I must wear sunscreen while I play.

Story

It was a hot and sunny Labor Day. Evan wanted to go out to play. It was the last holiday before school. He put on his sunscreen and a hat. Then he went to play with his friends.

❶ What does Dan want?

❷ What does he goes out

❸ How are the the story ali

1. Dan wants Jean to come out and play.

2. Evan puts on sunscreen and a hat before going out.

3. Both are about going out to play; it is Labor Day in both; the children in both wear sunscreen before going out to play.

128

© Scholastic, Inc.

FOR OUTSTANDING ACHIEVEMENT

CONGRATULATIONS!

This certificate is awarded to

I'm proud of you!

663264